Easthampstead Park

First Facts

All about Mountains

DONNA BAILEY

M

Macmillan

How to use this book

This book tells you lots of things about mountains. There is a list of Contents on the next page. It shows you what each double page of the book is about. For example, pages 6 and 7 tell you about 'Making mountains'.

On all of these pages you will find some words that are printed in **bold** type. The bold type shows you that these words are in the Glossary on pages 46 and 47. The Glossary explains the meaning of some words which may be new to you.

At the very end of the book there is an Index. The Index tells you where to find certain words in the book. For example, you can use it to look up words like fold mountains, glaciers, weathering and many other words to do with mountains.

Material used in this book first appeared in Macmillan World Library: *Mountains*.
Published by Macmillan Children's Books
A division of MACMILLAN PUBLISHERS LTD
Houndmills, Basingstoke, Hampshire RG21 2XS
and London
Companies and representatives throughout the world

Printed in Hong Kong

British Library Cataloguing in Publication Data
Bailey, Donna
All about mountains
1. Mountains – – For children
I. Title   II. Series
551.4'32

ISBN 0-333-49313-3

Contents

Introduction

Mountains reach up into the sky and are the highest parts of the land. They usually occur in **ranges**. The highest mountain range in the world is the Himalayas, and the highest mountain is Mount Everest. It is part of the Himalayas.

**looking
after llamas
in Peru**

People and animals live on
the slopes of mountains.
They need to keep warm and
shelter from the cold wind.
   This boy lives in the
high Andes Mountains.
His llamas have wool which
people weave into cloth
to make warm clothes.
   This grizzly bear has
thick fur to keep it warm.

a grizzly in Alaska

5

Making mountains

The Earth has four layers, with the
inner and outer **core** at its centre.
Around the core is a layer
of heavy rock called the **mantle**.
The thin outer layer of the mantle is
the Earth's **crust** which is made up of
huge pieces called **plates**.

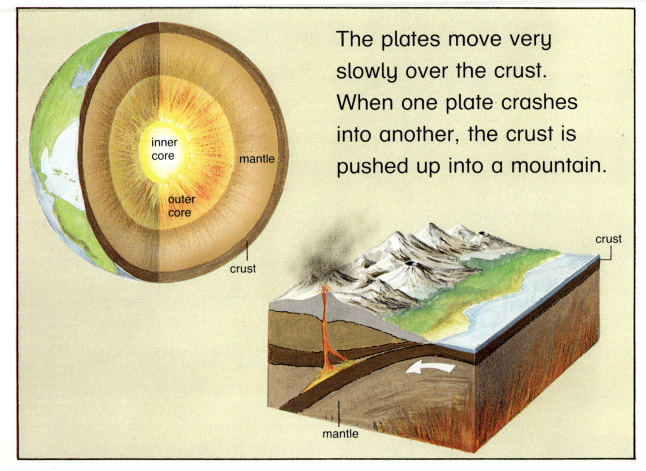

The plates move very
slowly over the crust.
When one plate crashes
into another, the crust is
pushed up into a mountain.

inner
core

mantle

outer
core

crust

crust

mantle

folds of rock in a cliff on the coast

Sometimes when two plates crash together, the ocean bed between two **continents** is pushed upwards. When this happens, huge folds of rock are pushed up to form mountains called **fold mountains**.

Where parts of the Earth's crust are weak, cracks or **faults** are made. Sometimes parts of the crust sink, leaving the rest standing above them. At other times parts of the Earth's crust are pushed upwards at a fault. Mountains made like this are called **block mountains** because they are made up of huge blocks of the Earth's crust.

how block mountains are made

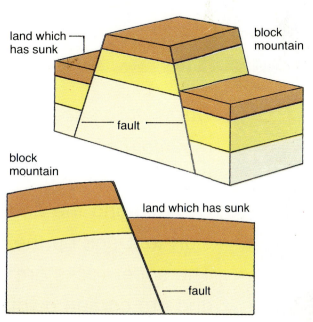

land which has sunk

block mountain

fault

block mountain

land which has sunk

fault

Weather, water and wind

Our picture shows Ayer's Rock, a
mountain which has changed shape over
thousands of years by **weathering**.
Ice, rain and the heat of the sun
start to break up the rocks.
The softer rocks are broken up first
and are carried away by **erosion**.

Rocks are most often eroded by water.

As the water drains off the mountain side it finds the easiest way down. The water builds up into a fast-flowing mountain stream, which flows down to the valley floor below. The stream takes pieces of rock and sand with it. These help to wear away the softer pieces of rock in the ground beneath the running stream. The stream cuts into the mountain, making a V-shaped valley.

Sometimes a stream flows over harder rock which it cannot cut through. It pours over this hard rock, making a waterfall.

On the way down the mountain, streams may join together to make a much bigger river.

At the foot of the mountain the land gets flatter, so the river flows more slowly. At the river mouth it drops the soil and stones it has been carrying.

a V-shaped valley

Rivers of ice

Glaciers are rivers of ice.
They start high up in the mountains
where it is very cold, and move
slowly down the mountain, carrying
stones and trees as they go.

a glacier at
Chamonix, in
France

a U-shaped valley made by a glacier

Thousands of years ago when the Earth's weather was colder than it is now, huge sheets of ice covered parts of the continents. The ice moved in huge glaciers which made many of the U-shaped valleys like the one in our picture.

In some places glaciers cut right into the sea bed. When the weather became warmer the ice melted.

Norwegian fiords were made by glaciers

When the ice melted, long narrow areas of deep water called **fiords** were left.

11

Mountain weather

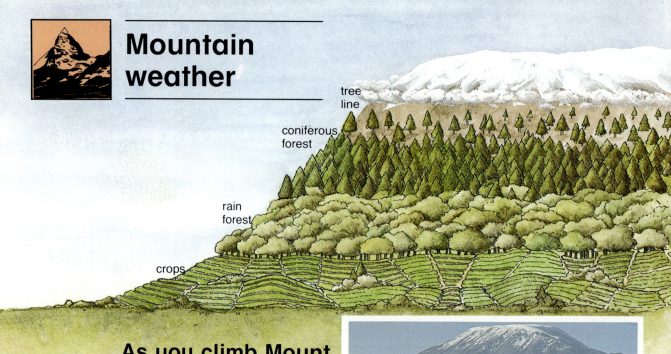

tree line

coniferous forest

rain forest

crops

As you climb Mount Kilimanjaro, the climate changes as you get higher up.

Mount Kilimanjaro is near the **Equator**.
It rises up from a hot dry plain.
Rain falls on the lower slopes of the mountain, and crops grow well there.
Higher up there is warm, wet **rain forest**, but above that the **climate** becomes colder and drier.
This is the **coniferous forest** level.
No trees grow above the **tree line**.

Our picture shows the lower slopes of
a mountain in the Alps, where animals
can graze on the long grass in summer.
Higher up there are forests, and then
the trees get fewer and smaller.

Above the tree line the air is thin
and there is little water because
the rain freezes and falls as snow.

Plants that grow at this level have
to be very tough to survive.
Alpine plants put down long roots in
the cracks between the rocks.

Mountain animals

Animals which live in the mountains above the tree line have **adapted** to living so high up.
Some have large hearts and **lungs** to breathe the thin mountain air and thick fur to keep their bodies warm.
They must also be good at climbing.

Birds in the mountains have strong, broad wings to fly in high winds.

This condor lives in the Andes. It glides over the high mountains and looks out for dead animals to eat. It can fly up to a height of 7000 m and can still see the ground below very clearly.

Staying alive

In winter, it is very cold in the
mountains and it is hard for the
animals to **survive**.

The yaks that live in the mountains
of Tibet have very thick coats.
In winter, a yak's coat is so long it
almost touches the ground.
The yaks eat mosses and **lichens** when
they cannot find grass under the snow.
They live at 6000 m above sea level.

This Rocky mountain goat also lives
in the mountains above the tree line.
It has thick hair to keep it warm and
eats mosses when it can't find grass.

Some animals change the colour of
their fur to match the surroundings.

The stoat changes its colour in
winter from brown to white, so that
it can creep up on its prey without
being seen in the snow.

Mountains like walls

Mountains act as **barriers**. They make natural walls to stop plants and animals spreading from one area to another.

Mountains also affect the climate of a country. Rain falls on the Great Dividing Range in Australia but the mountains stop the winds that carry rain from moving into the middle of the continent.

In Asia, mountains divide the south of the continent from the north. Warm, wet **monsoon** winds blow in the south, but the lands on the northern side are dry and cold.

a mountain plant

the Great Dividing Range

18

Dall sheep in Canada

Huge mountain chains run
from north to south along
the west coast of North
and South America.
Animals live in a climate
above the tree line in
these mountains that does
not change for hundreds of
kilometres.
The Dall sheep in our
picture lives in the high
Rocky Mountains in Canada.

19

Mountains of fire

Volcanoes are holes or **vents** in the
Earth's crust which lead down to the
mantle deep inside the Earth.
Some of the mantle is not solid rock,
but liquid rock called **magma**.
Sometimes hot gases and magma
push their way up through a vent.
When this happens, a volcano **erupts**.

**a volcano
erupting in
Hawaii**

The hot magma that is pushed out is called **lava**. Rocks and hot ash are also thrown up in an eruption. The rocks and ash pile up to make a mountain around the vent.

The shape and size of a volcano depends on if the lava is thick or runny. A steep–sided cone volcano has thick sticky lava. A shield volcano which has thin runny lava is large and flat.

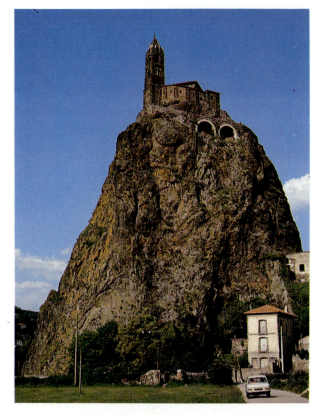

this hill in France was once a volcano

These cone volcanoes are made from layers of sticky lava and ash.

The lava from a shield volcano pours out in a thin stream.

21

Two famous eruptions

Mount St Helens exploded in 1980.
It had been sending out gas, steam
and ash for three months beforehand.
The gas that could not escape built
up inside the mountain.
During the eruption one side of the
mountain blew out, sending out a
blast of hot gases, steam and ash.
Farmlands were buried, rivers were
blocked and many people died.

When people in Paricutin, Mexico, saw
ash coming from a crack in the ground
they did not know it was a volcano.
The mounds of ash and rock grew higher
and covered their farms and houses.
The lava even buried a nearby village,
except for the top of its church.

The Ring of Fire

Our map shows that many active volcanoes are ringed around the Pacific Ocean in the Ring of Fire.

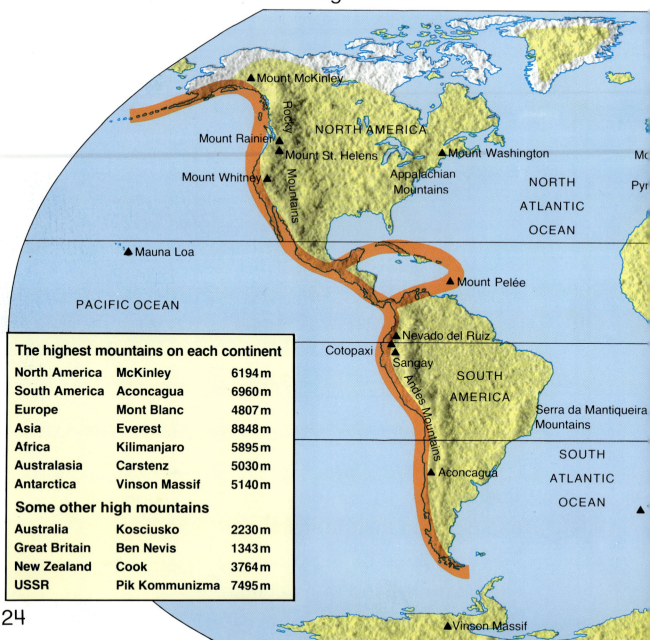

▲Mount McKinley

NORTH AMERICA

Rocky Mountains

Mount Rainier▲
▲Mount St. Helens
▲Mount Washington

Mount Whitney▲

Appalachian Mountains

NORTH ATLANTIC OCEAN

Pyr

Mc

▲Mauna Loa

PACIFIC OCEAN

▲Mount Pelée

▲Nevado del Ruiz
Cotopaxi
Sangay

SOUTH AMERICA

Andes Mountains

Serra da Mantiqueira Mountains

SOUTH ATLANTIC OCEAN

▲Aconcagua

▲Vinson Massif

The highest mountains on each continent		
North America	McKinley	6194 m
South America	Aconcagua	6960 m
Europe	Mont Blanc	4807 m
Asia	Everest	8848 m
Africa	Kilimanjaro	5895 m
Australasia	Carstenz	5030 m
Antarctica	Vinson Massif	5140 m
Some other high mountains		
Australia	Kosciusko	2230 m
Great Britain	Ben Nevis	1343 m
New Zealand	Cook	3764 m
USSR	Pik Kommunizma	7495 m

The volcanoes are found where the plates
of the Earth's crust rub together, or
where they are moving apart.
These parts of the Earth's crust are
weaker and magma pushes to the surface
and erupts.

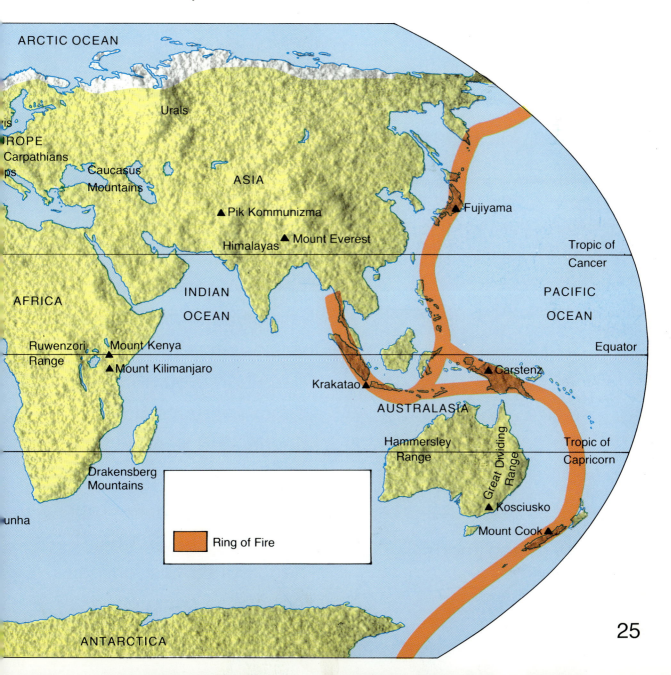

ARCTIC OCEAN

Urals

is

ROPE

Carpathians

ps

Caucasus
Mountains

ASIA

▲ Pik Kommunizma

Himalayas ▲ Mount Everest

▲ Fujiyama

Tropic of
Cancer

INDIAN

OCEAN

PACIFIC

OCEAN

AFRICA

Equator

Ruwenzori ▲ Mount Kenya
Range

▲ Mount Kilimanjaro

Krakatao ▲

▲ Carstenz

AUSTRALASIA

Hammersley
Range

Great Dividing Range

Tropic of

Capricorn

Drakensberg
Mountains

▲ Kosciusko

unha

Mount Cook ▲

Ring of Fire

ANTARCTICA

25

The Andes

The Andes are a range of mountains along the west coast of South America. Many years ago the Inca people lived there in the country now called Peru.

the land of the Incas

The Incas were rich and powerful people.
They built houses from blocks of stone.
They built roads between their towns in zig zags up the steep mountain slopes.
They shared out the land so that everyone had enough land to grow food.
The farmers cut huge steps or **terraces** to grow crops of maize and potatoes.
They kept llamas for their wool and to carry goods.

Our picture shows Quechua Indians who
live in the Andes today and still
plough the land and plant potatoes
just like the Incas in the past.
Their way of life has changed very
little for hundreds of years.
They still live in stone houses in
the mountains.
They keep llamas and alpacas to
eat their meat and use their wool.
The Indians dye the wool into bright
colours and use the dyed wool to
weave patterns in their cloth.

Mountain hideouts

People who live in mountains are often cut off from the rest of the world because the mountains act as a barrier.

These people live in dense forest in the mountains of Papua New Guinea. Travel is hard in the mountains and the people have few visitors. Their way of life has not changed for hundreds of years.

living in Papua New Guinea

a mountain village in Lesotho

Some people choose to live in the mountains because they can be safer there. The people of Lesotho made their homes in the Drakensberg Mountains to escape from their enemies.

This **monastery** in Greece was built at the top of a mountain for the monks to live in peace and quiet.

Crossing the mountains

When people want to cross a mountain
range they look for a pass.
This is a valley between two peaks.
To avoid making a mountain road too
steep, it is built through a pass
and not over the tops of mountains.
The road is built to follow the
natural curves of the valley.

Our picture shows the road through
the Khyber Pass across the mountains
between Afghanistan and Pakistan.

The settlers in America travelled
across the continent from east to
west, on horseback and in wagons.
There were no roads then, and travel
across the high mountains of the
Rockies was difficult and dangerous.
Sometimes the wagons had to go along
narrow ledges with a steep drop on
one side and falling rocks above.
Food was hard to find, and many of
the settlers did not survive the journey.

Life in the mountains

The Sherpa people of Nepal are used to living high up in the Himalayas. These Sherpas are gathering firewood for cooking and to heat their homes.

Sherpas can carry heavy loads in the thin mountain air, when other people would become breathless. Sherpas often work carrying loads for mountaineers in the Himalayas.

a Swiss village

These Sherpas are buying cloth in the market. They nearly all wear hats and have many layers of clothes to keep warm.

Sherpa houses have small windows to help keep the houses warm in winter.

Houses in Switzerland have long sloping roofs which hang over the walls. The sloping roof stops the snow from blocking the doors and windows. People store firewood against the walls under the roofs to keep it dry.

a Sherpa village

33

People and animals

People who live in the mountains keep
animals for food and for their wool.
Animals can also carry goods.

These Quechua Indians in Peru use
llamas to carry their loads.
The woman on the right is spinning
llama wool into thread for cloth.

Many mountain farmers keep goats
because they can eat most plants.

People in the Himalayas keep yaks.
They burn dried yak dung for fuel.

These cows spend the summer eating
grass high up in the Swiss Alps.
The herdsmen live in huts near them.
In the winter the herdsmen take the
cows down to the valley.
There the animals are kept indoors
where it is warm and dry.

Farming in the mountains

The soil in the mountains is poor and the summers are often short.
Farmers grow crops on the lower slopes.

picking tea in Japan

When farmers want to grow crops in
the mountains they have to make sure
the plants get enough water.
It is also more difficult to plant
crops on mountain slopes rather than
on flat land.
People make fields out of terraces
that they cut in the mountain sides.
   Our picture shows rice being grown
on terraces in the Philippines.

Using mountains

Some mountains are covered in forests.
The wood from the trees is used to
make houses and furniture.

There are **minerals** such as gold,
silver and iron in some mountains.
Our picture shows Mount Tom Price in
Australia which is made of iron ore.
The mountain is slowly disappearing as
the iron ore is mined and taken away.

People also use the water which rushes
down from the mountain rivers.

A strong wall or **dam** is built across
the river so the water is held back to
make a lake or **reservoir**.
The water in the reservoir can be
used to make electricity.
When a small gate in the dam is opened,
the water rushes through and turns a
turbine to make the electricity.
Our picture shows the Glen Canyon Dam
which holds water from the Rockies.

Travel in the mountains

People can build roads in zig zags
up the steep sides of mountains.
There are sharp bends in these roads.
In winter the roads can get blocked
by snow and ice.
Then they are cleared by snow ploughs.
When the roads are icy, drivers can
wrap chains around the wheels of
their cars to grip the road better.

a mountain road

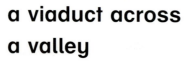

**a viaduct across
a valley**

the Central Line in Peru

Trains cannot go up very steep slopes, so the tracks must be kept as level as possible.

Trains can go through tunnels in the mountains, and across bridges called **viaducts** which cross over the valleys.

The Central Line in Peru which runs from the coast up into the Andes has 66 tunnels and 59 bridges. The line zig zags on ledges up the steep mountain slopes. The train goes very high. There the air is thin and people sometimes find it hard to breathe!

Mountain sports

Many people enjoy mountain holidays.
Some people like walking, but many
like to ride to the top of a mountain
in a **cable car** to enjoy the view.
This cable car is taking tourists to
the top of Sugar Loaf Mountain in Rio
de Janeiro, Brazil.

learning to ski

Some people spend their winter holidays skiing. Many mountain villages are centres for skiing holidays. Cable cars or ski lifts take the skiers to the top of the ski runs.

Other people go rock climbing. They need special clothes and equipment.

climbing Mont Blanc

The magic of the mountains

Mountains are very special places.
High mountain ranges are parts of the
world that have not been spoiled, so
animals can live there in peace.
There are now laws to stop people from
hunting animals like the snow leopard.
This animal nearly died out because
people hunted it for its fur.

Some countries are making their mountain areas into national parks where animals can live.

Mountains are often very beautiful places. Mount Fujiyama in Japan is a perfect cone shape. Some people believe that the mountain is a holy place.

back-packing in Jasper National Park

Mount Fujiyama

Glossary

adapted   changed in order to suit different surroundings

Alpine   plants and animals that are used to living high up in the Alps

barriers   objects that keep people or animals apart

block mountains   mountains made when a part of the Earth's outer shell is pushed up and stands above the surrounding land

cable car   a cabin hung from cables which carries people up the sides of mountains

climate   the weather of a particular area

coniferous forest   forest made up of trees which keep their leaves all year round

continents   large pieces of land which may contain many countries. The Earth is divided into seven continents.

core   the centre of the Earth

crust   the outer shell of the Earth

dam   a strong wall built to hold back a river

Equator   the imaginary circle which goes round the middle of the Earth. The hottest parts of the world are nearest the Equator

erosion   the wearing away of land by water, ice and wind

erupt   to send out liquid rock, smoke and ashes

faults   cracks in the outer shell of the Earth

fiords   long narrow pieces of sea between high cliffs or mountains

fold mountains   mountains made when the outer shell of the Earth is wrinkled up

glaciers   slow-moving rivers of ice

lava   hot, liquid rock that flows from deep inside the Earth. The lava cools and hardens when it comes to the surface.

lichens   slow-growing plants that can live on very little food and water

lungs   parts of our bodies inside our chests, used for breathing

magma   melted rock beneath the Earth's crust

mantle   a layer of the Earth that lies between the outer shell and the central core

minerals   materials dug from the Earth by mining

monastery   a place where
monks live, work and pray

monsoon   a strong wind that
blows in South East Asia,
bringing heavy rain

plates   sections of the Earth's
outer shell, which float on the
surface of the liquid rock
beneath

rain forest   forest with large
leaved trees which grow in warm
wet climates

ranges   lines of mountains

reservoir   a lake which builds up
behind a dam to collect and hold
water

survive   to stay alive

terraces   wide, level steps cut
into a mountain side for growing
crops

tree line   the upper limit that
trees will grow on a mountain

turbine   a wheel with many
curved blades which is turned by
the flow of water. Turbines drive
machines which make electricity.

vents   openings in the outer
shell of the Earth that lead down
to the liquid rock beneath. A
volcano forms around a vent.

viaducts   long, high bridges
across a valley

weathering   the action of
weather on rock. Wind, rain, ice
and heat wear away the surface
of the rock, or break it up

Index

Acknowledgements
The Publishers wish to thank the following organizations for their invaluable assistance in the preparation of this book.
Canadian High Commission
Swiss National Tourist Office
Photographic credits
(*t=top b=bottom l=left r=right*)
Cover photograph: Robert Harding Picture Library; title page Robert Harding Picture Library
4 ZEFA; 5*t* South American Pictures; 5*b* John Waters/Seaphot; 7*t* J. G. James/Seaphot; 8 Ed Rotberg; 9 The Hutchison Library; 10 Douglas Dickens; 11*t* The Hutchison Library; 11*b* Douglas Dickens; 12, 13 ZEFA; 14 Claudio Galasso/Seaphot; 15 South American Pictures; 16 The Hutchison Library; 17 Franz Camenzind/Seaphot; 18 R. J. Hart; 18/19 R. & D. Keller/NHPA; 19 Ivor Edmonds/Seaphot; 20 ZEFA; 21 Douglas Dickens; 22 ZEFA; 23, 26 South American Pictures; 27 The Hutchison Library; 28, 29*t* ZEFA; 29*b*, 30 Douglas Dickens; 32, 33*t*, 33*b* ZEFA; 34 Douglas Dickens; 35 Swiss National Tourist Office; 36*t* John Lythgoe/Seaphot; 36*b* Douglas Dickens; 37, 38 ZEFA; 39 Ardea; 40 ZEFA; 40/41 Swiss National Tourist Office; 41 South American Pictures; 42, 43*t*, 43*b* ZEFA; 44 Ardea; 45*t* Canadian High Commission, 45*b* ZEFA